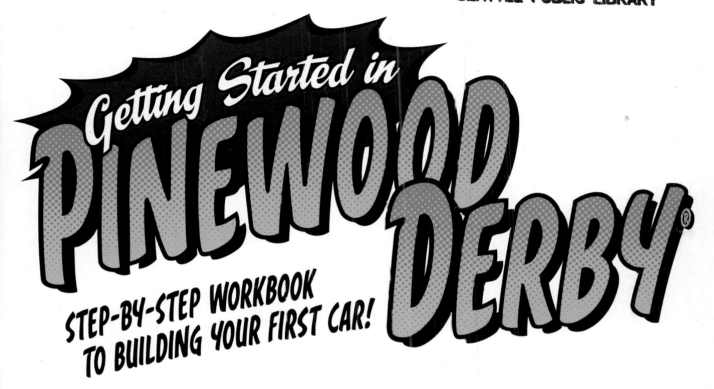

Getting Started in PINEWOOD DERBY®

STEP-BY-STEP WORKBOOK TO BUILDING YOUR FIRST CAR!

Getting Started in PINEWOOD DERBY®

STEP-BY-STEP WORKBOOK TO BUILDING YOUR FIRST CAR!

TROY THORNE

FOX CHAPEL
PUBLISHING

Dedication

I dedicate this book with love and thanks to my family: My wife Beth, who has stuck with me through everything, and my three children, Nathan, Kelsey, and Camryn. And, to my parents and grandfather, for teaching me to try anything. You all make it possible for me to pursue my ideas, while putting up with all the headaches of the big projects I get involved in.

ISBN 978-1-56523-617-2

To learn more about the other great books from Fox Chapel Publishing, or to find a retailer near you, call toll-free 800-457-9112 or visit us at *www.FoxChapelPublishing.com*.

Note to Authors: We are always looking for talented authors to write new books in our area of woodworking, design, and related crafts. Please send a brief letter describing your idea to Acquisition Editor, 1970 Broad Street, East Petersburg, PA 17520.

Printed in China
First printing: 2011

Publisher's Cataloging-in-Publication Data

Thorne, Troy.

Getting started in Pinewood Derby : step-by-step workbook to building your first car / Troy Thorne. -- East Petersburg, PA : Fox Chapel Publishing, c2011.

p. : ill. ; cm.

ISBN: 978-1-56523-617-2

Summary: Designed to help parents and children enjoy building a simple Boy Scouts Pinewood Derby car together, especially if they have no woodworking skills. Photo-illustrated step-by-step instructions, materials lists, and patterns make the process easy to understand.

1. Model car racing--Juvenile literature. 2. Automobiles, Racing--Models--Design and construction--Juvenile literature. 3. [Automobiles--Models--Design and construction. 4. Model car racing. 5. Automobiles, Racing--Models--Design and construction.] I. Title.

GV1570 .T464 2011

796.15/6--dc22 1109

About the Author

Creative Director, woodworker, and Assistant Scoutmaster Troy Thorne has helped to build hundreds of derby cars. He participates in Scouting activities with his son, Nathan, who was a national finalist in the All-Star Derby Design Contest. Nate has grown out of Cub Scouts and is on his way to Eagle, but luckily Troy's daughter, Kelsey, is racing Awana cars. Troy's latest project is a street-legal AC Cobra replica.

Dear Adventurers,

I'd like you to meet Dash Derby. He will be your tour guide through the process of building a derby car. His character is part me, and part all the kids I've worked with making hundreds of derby cars over the past ten years. The part of him that comes from me likes red, and especially likes cool cars! Follow along with Dash and you'll be able to make an awesome derby car, too!

– Troy

TABLE OF CONTENTS

Cool Stuff For Kids! 8

Boring Stuff For Mom and Dad 9

Getting Started 10

Session 1: Shopping 22

Session 2: Shaping 26

Session 3: Painting 36

Session 4: Axle Prep 52

Session 5: Wheel Prep 56

Session 6: Weighting 60

Session 7: Test Runs 66

Race Day Tips 74

Memories 76

Patterns 80

Index 94

Cool Stuff for Kids!

HI, KIDS! I'm Dash Derby, and I'll be your guide through the daring world of Pinewood Derby racing. This book is designed so the larger process of building a car is split into seven smaller pieces. As you progress through the Seven Steps, be sure to take your time. A good idea would be to do one step each day, or one step every week. Set goals for yourself and stick to them—and you'll have an awesome car built in no time! Building a derby car is fun and exciting, but there are some ground rules you should follow.

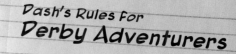

Dash's Rules for Derby Adventurers

1. Have **FUN!**

2. Don't wait until the last minute to get started.

3. If you get tired, stop.

4. Don't let your parents take over—this is your project.

5. The derby isn't about winning—it's about having fun and learning new skills along the way!

Boring Stuff for Mom and Dad

HI, ADULTS! If you and your child have never experienced the Pinewood Derby before, you've come to the right place. This book will guide you through the creation of a derby car from start to finish, explaining everything you need to know, WITHOUT overwhelming either of you.

We've broken down the process into seven easy chunks. These chunks can be approached one at a time. I recommend giving each step its own separate day; that way, your child can accomplish the tasks without getting tired or exasperated. If you create a schedule of accomplishing one or two of the steps a week, you can have your car done well in advance of race day.

The Pinewood Derby experience is a great way to spend quality time with your kid, and to allow him to develop a sense of pride in his own work. Work as a team, and don't be afraid to give your child the reins—after all, this is his project! It's impossible for your child to fully experience the Pinewood Derby if YOU build the car. Remember—the number one goal of the Derby is having fun!

I wish I could help build my car.

What NOT to do.

Don't find yourself in this situation. The car doesn't have to be perfect—it just needs to be your kid's!

GETTING STARTED

Embarking on the Amazing Adventure

Where do I start?

THE CHRONICLES OF DASH DERBY

Dear Adventurers,

Today I spent some time reading the materials that I gathered here in the next section for you. There's all sorts of useful information to get you on your way to creating an awesome derby car. I learned which tools I need, what safety equipment to use, and even about poison (check out the sidebar on page 14)! Mom said reading this stuff is like mentally preparing for a wild adventure—you've got to review your treasure map before you take your first step down the path. I thought that was pretty neat, so I decided to draw my own treasure map of the Seven Derby Steps!

Dash Derby's SEVEN DERBY STEPS!

Shopping, page 22

Shaping, page 26

Axle Prep, page 52

Session 1

Session 2

Session 3

Session 4

Painting, page 36

Session 5

Session 7

Race Day!!

Session 6

Wheel Prep, page 56

Weighting, page 60

Test Runs, page 66

Choosing a Design

This pattern is really cool, but I think it's too hard for me.

We've included a handful of cool car designs in the back of the book, starting on page 80. All of them are great first cars to work on. However, don't be afraid to modify the designs. As long as your car fits within the specifications of your local Derby, you can go wild! Just select a design that you like—we promise that all of the designs in this book can be created in real life by you!

As you gather the tools and materials for the building process, review the official and local Pinewood Derby rules and the Official Grand Prix Pinewood Derby car specifications. The list of suggested rules that accompanies each Official Grand Prix Pinewood Derby Kit® is shown at right and the specifications are illustrated below. If you don't have a copy of your local rules, ask your local race committee for one. Then abide by all of them. Remember, when you compete in the Pinewood Derby, be honest. If one of the designs in this book does not fit within your local Derby's rules, don't use it. If you are unsure whether something is legal, check with your local race organizer before you build the car.

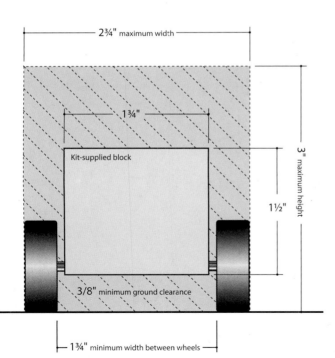

2¾" maximum width

1¾"

Kit-supplied block

3" maximum height

1½"

3/8" minimum ground clearance

1¾" minimum width between wheels

Official Pinewood Derby Rules

1 Wheel bearings and bushings are prohibited.

2 The car shall not ride on springs.

3 Only official Cub Scout Grand Prix Pinewood Derby wheels and axles are permitted.

4 Only dry lubricant is permitted.

5 Details, such as steering wheel and driver, are permissible as long as these details do not exceed the maximum length, width, and weight specifications.

6 The car must be free-wheeling, with no starting devices.

7 Each car must pass inspection by the official inspection committee before it may compete. If, at registration, a car does not pass inspection, the owner will be informed of the reason for failure and will be given time within the official weigh-in time period to make the adjustment. After approval, cars will not be re-inspected unless the car is damaged in handling or in a race.

Safety

Safety is the number one tool in an experienced Adventurer's bag of tricks. It is very important to be mindful of your fingers and body parts to avoid injuries—make sure that your fingers are not in the path of a saw blade or sanding pad. There are a few pieces of safety equipment that will help you: a dust mask, safety glasses, and ear protection. Wear a dust mask to protect against harmful fumes and airborne particles when you're sanding, applying graphite, and spray painting. Form the metal strip at the top of the mask over your nose to create a tight seal.

Eye protection is very important when sanding wood and working with power tools. Wear some safety glasses or goggles to make sure no stray bits of wood find their way into your eyes. Power drills, band saws, and sanders can make loud buzzing noises that hurt your ears. You can find earplugs and headphone-style ear muffs at home centers in the lawn care or safety section.

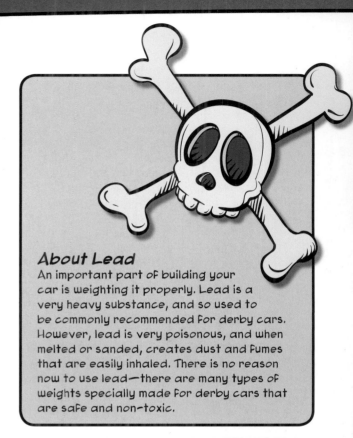

About Lead

An important part of building your car is weighting it properly. Lead is a very heavy substance, and so used to be commonly recommended for derby cars. However, lead is very poisonous, and when melted or sanded, creates dust and fumes that are easily inhaled. There is no reason now to use lead—there are many types of weights specially made for derby cars that are safe and non-toxic.

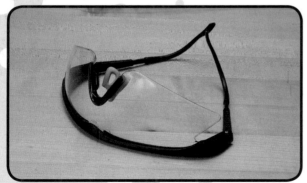

Safety Glasses
Eye protection is very important when sanding wood and working with power tools. Invest in safety glasses or goggles that protect your eyes and your child's eyes from the front and the sides.

Dust Masks
Wear dust masks to protect against harmful fumes and airborne particles when sanding, applying graphite, and spray painting. Form the metal strip at the top of the mask over the bridge of your nose to create a tight seal.

Workspace

If your parents have a workshop in the garage or basement, that is a fantastic spot to build a derby car. If not, the kitchen or picnic table is just as good. If you're not working in a designated shop area, just make sure to cover your work surface with newspaper. When it comes time to do test runs, the spare leaf in the dining room table makes a great test track.

Power Tool Workshop Day

Most Boy Scout packs have a power tool day in the weeks before the Derby race. It is a great idea to take advantage of this if you are interested in learning how to use cool tools—like band saws, scroll saws, power drills, and power sanders—with the help of someone experienced.

This way, you can also avoid needing to purchase power tools if you don't have much other use for them. Plus, it's always fun to work on your car with other kids; you never know who will have a great idea to volunteer.

Ear Protection
Ear protection is necessary whenever you run power equipment. Ear protection is available at home centers in the lawn care or the safety section.

Tools You May Need

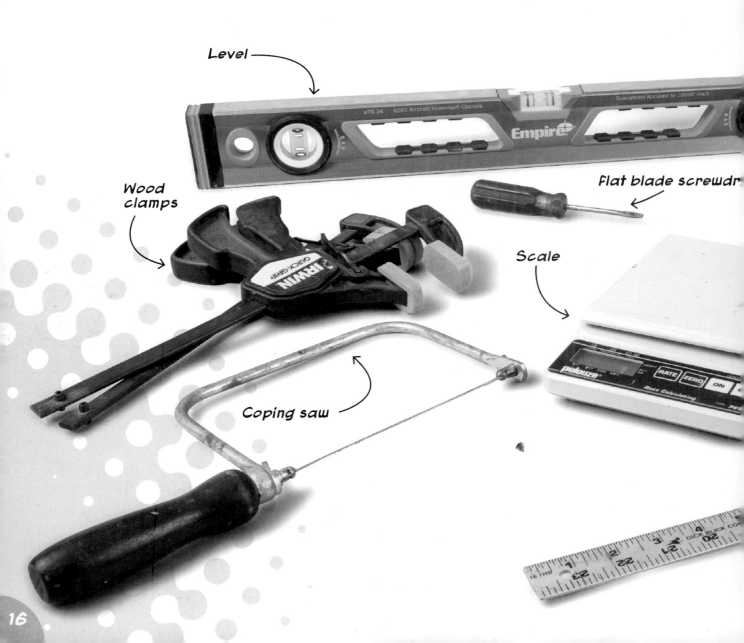

Level

Flat blade screwdr

Wood clamps

Scale

Coping saw

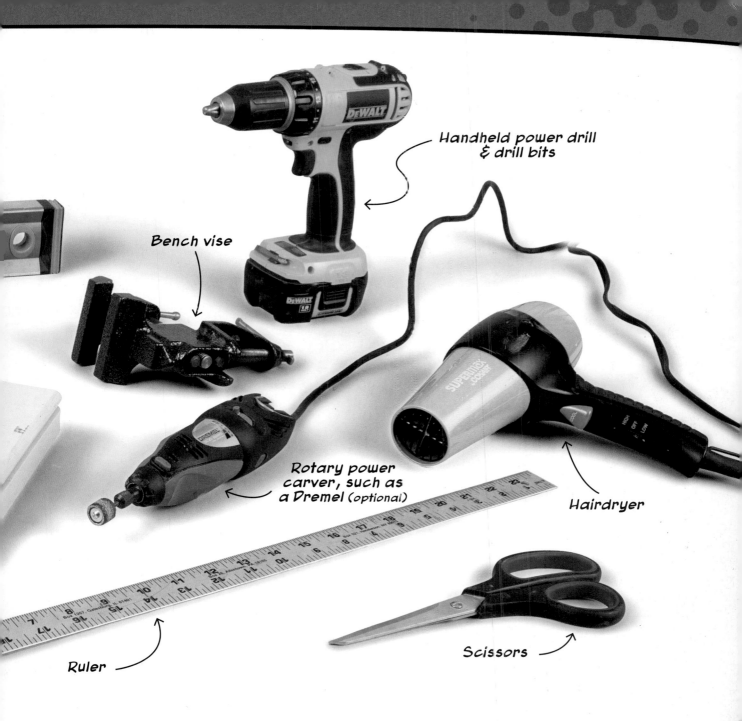

Handheld power drill & drill bits

Bench vise

Rotary power carver, such as a Dremel (optional)

Hairdryer

Ruler

Scissors

Coping Saw Skills — The Straight Cut

Using a coping saw is a fun way for you to remove wood from the block yourself. Make sure you read the next few pages carefully before you pick up a saw. After you understand how to use a coping saw, you can make your car any shape you want! The first step is learning how to do a straight cut. If you have trouble getting the saw started, make a few short cuts at first—don't try to use the whole length of the saw blade.

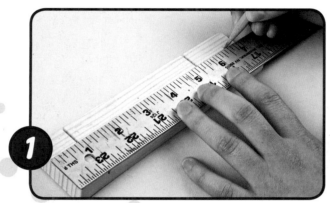

Make a mark.
Mark the point where you want the straight line to be. Use a ruler to make a straight line where your mark is.

Prepare the vise.
Use painter's tape to stick a thin piece of scrap wood to both jaws of the vise. This will prevent crunching the piece you're cutting.

Clamp the wood.
Place the wood between the jaws of the vise and gently tighten the vise until the wood is secure. Be sure to leave a few inches of space between the cutting path and the vise.

Cut the line.
Hold the saw handle with your dominant hand. Use your other hand to hold the piece steady, or to guide the other end of the saw. Keep the saw blade level and straight from the front to the back.

Coping Saw Skills — The Curved Cut

Making a curved cut with the coping saw is pretty similar to making a straight cut. You still need to pay attention, go slowly, and keep the saw blade straight through the entire cut. The biggest difference is you're likely to need to move the hoop of the saw out of the way. Luckily, that is pretty easy—most coping saws have a twist fastener that lets you orient the blade however you want.

1

Clamp the wood.
Put the piece of wood between the jaws of the vise so you can get to the area you need to cut.

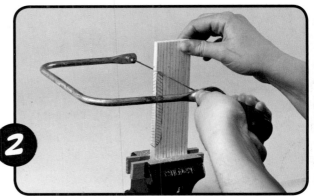

2

Start the cut.
When you get to a spot where you can't saw without hitting the hoop of the saw on the wood, remove the saw from the cut.

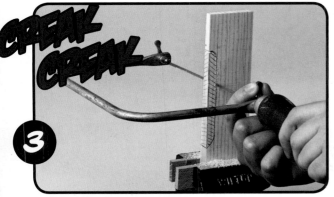

3

Move the hoop.
Loosen the blade and twist the hoop so it's out of the way. Retighten the blade and continue sawing.

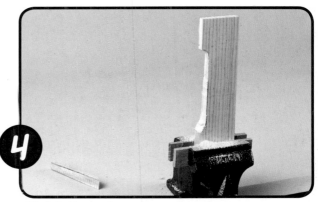

4

Finish the cut.
Keep sawing until you've finished your cut. If you need to readjust the hoop again, stop and do it.

Coping Saw Skills — The Notched Cut

The hardest part about making a notched cut is getting sharp corners. You can't cut right down and make a 90° turn, or the blade will snap. You need to think about it a bit differently. How about cutting a curve instead?

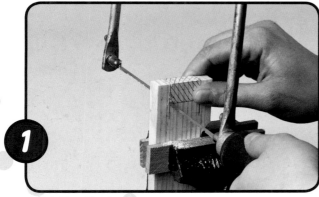

Cut the first side.
Clamp the wood so you can saw comfortably. Saw down one side to the bottom corner.

Cut the second side.
Saw down the second side to the bottom corner.

Cut a curve.
On one side, make a second cut to remove a little more wood. Now you have enough room to rotate the blade and start cutting down toward the other corner.

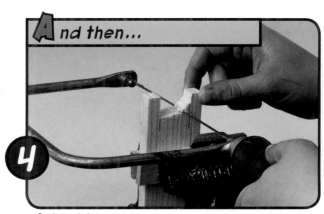

And then...

Cut out the corner.
With that big piece removed, now you can come back for the last corner. Make the flat cut on the bottom and it should fall free.

Coping Saw Skills — The Internal Cut

An internal cut is when you cut out a shape that is completely surrounded by wood. It is a hole through the car. It's a cool-looking effect that doesn't take much more effort than making a straight cut—you just have to have your mom or dad help you drill to get started.

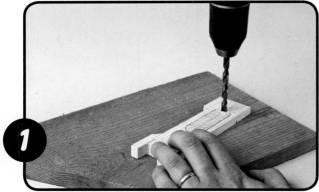

1

Drill an entry hole.
Ask an adult to drill an entry hole for you near the outline of the shape. Remind the adult to drill on a piece of scrap wood.

2

Clamp the wood.
Unfasten the blade and poke it through the hole in the wood. Hook up the blade to the saw again, and you're ready to go!

3

Saw on the lines.
Follow the lines you drew and cut out the piece.

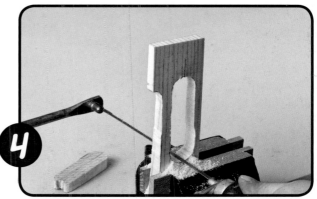

4

Knock out the piece.
When you have cut the whole way around, poke out the piece with your finger.

SESSION 1
SHOPPING
A Monumental Quest For Stupendous Stuff!

THE CHRONICLES OF DASH DERBY

Dear Adventurers,

Today, Mom and Dad took me on a car ride to the store. I brought a big list of stuff I needed (there's a copy of it on the next page). It was really fun going up and down all the aisles, looking for all the pieces I needed to make my awesome derby car. The cashier was funny, and told us this joke when I said I was building a derby car: What happened to the frog's car when it broke down? It got toad away!

The Hardware Store List

☐ Sandpaper assortment (100, 150, 220)
☐ Wet or dry sandpaper (400, 600)
☐ Paper towels
☐ Painter's masking tape
☐ Wood putty (optional, just in case)
☐ Foam brush
☐ White glue
☐ Glue stick

The Craft Store List

☐ Decoration – Choose one or more
    ☐ Acrylic paints (see page 36)
    ☐ Permanent markers (see page 43)
    ☐ Decorative paper (see page 44)
☐ Paintbrush
☐ 1" Foam brushes
☐ Popsicle sticks
☐ Pencil

The Hobby Shop or Online List

☐ Pinewood Derby kit
☐ Wheel mandrel
☐ Graphite, such as Hob-E-Lube
☐ Colored derby wheels (optional)
☐ Decals or stickers
☐ Acrylic paint
☐ Pinstripe tape (Auto parts store)
☐ Weights – Choose one or more
    ☐ Split shot (Fishing departments)
    ☐ Round weight bars
    ☐ Stick-on weights
    ☐ Combo weights
    ☐ Plate weight

Which Weight?

There are many types of weights you can use. My favorite combination is split shot and a plate weight. Depending on the car design you choose, certain weights will work better than others. For example, if you have a design where the center of the car is cut away, you wouldn't want a weight plate—it would hide the cool hole you made. If you and your parent are comfortable drilling, you can use split shot and round weights. If you don't like drilling, try stick-on weights or combo weights. Remember, most weights will snap apart into smaller sections so you can make sure your car weighs the right amount.

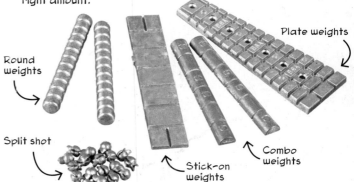

Round weights

Plate weights

Split shot

Stick-on weights

Combo weights

SHOPPING

Stuff You May Need

Glue

Glue stick

Colored derby wheels

Pinewood Derby kit

GRAND PRIX
PINEWOOD
WHEELS

ELMER'S
CRAFT

Extra
Strength
Glue Stick

ELMER'S
Washable, No Run
School
Glue
Safe, Non-Toxic

CUB SCOUT
DERBY
GRAND PRIX
PINEWOOD
DERBY KIT

BSA

Painter's
tape

Regular
sandpaper

Wheel mandrel

100
150
220

Split
shot

Popsicle
sticks

Pinstripe
tape

3M
Imperial
Wetordry
Sandpaper
Imperial
Wetordry
Papel de lija

600

Car weights

Permanent
markers

Wet or dry
sandpaper

DRY GRAPHITE LUBRICANT
WITH MOLYBDENUM
IDEAL LUBRICANT FOR PINECAR RACERS • R/C MODELS

Graphite

Stainable Wood Filler

Use wet or dry for a premiere finish on
lacquers, primers, sealers, plastics and paints
Utilice seca o mojada para acabados en lacas,
primers, selladores, plásticos ó pinturas.

5   3²/₃ in/pulg x 9 in/pulg
Cont.: 5 Hojas de 93,1 mm x 228 mm   5921ES

Wood putty

Paper towels

Scrapbook paper

rylic paint

Foam brushes

Paint brush

Pencil

Decals

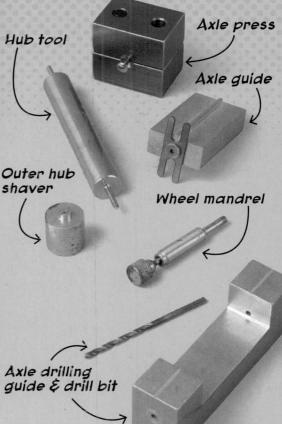

Special Derby Tools

These tools are available online and at hobby stores. They are specially designed tools that will help your construction go really well, and they will help you get every bit of speed out of your car. But my dad says you don't need them to make a car. The only tool you really need the first year is the wheel mandrel. Maybe next year, after I've got the basic stuff down, I'll try these advanced tools!

Hub tool

Axle press

Axle guide

Outer hub shaver

Wheel mandrel

Axle drilling guide & drill bit

SESSION 2
SHAPING
The Incredible Transformation From Block to Legend

That's awesome!

THE CHRONICLES OF DASH DERBY

Hey Adventurers!

Today I shaped my wood block into something that actually looked like the car I wanted! I learned about measuring, and marking, and even got to use sandpaper. Dad said if I wasn't careful, I could sand off my head, but I think he was just kidding. You can't sand off your head with just sandpaper, right? Anyway, it's really cool to see the car taking shape! Have Fun, and remember to measure twice and cut once—trust me, if you mess up it takes too much time to Fix!

Materials & Tool List...

- ☐ Pinewood derby kit
- ☐ Pencil
- ☐ Ruler
- ☐ Wood clamps
- ☐ Coping saw
- ☐ Sandpaper (100 Grit)
- ☐ Sandpaper (150 Grit)
- ☐ Painter's masking tape
- ☐ Elbow grease

1

Mark the Front of the car.
The axle notches aren't equal. The Front has more space between the notch and the Front. Be sure to mark it clearly!

2

Mark the height of the Front.
On the Front of the car, measure ¼" up From the bottom and make a mark.

3

Mark the top point of the wedge.
Mark 1" From the bottom of the back of the car to mark the back point of the wedge.

4

Draw the wedge angle.
Connect the two points to create the profile of the wedge.

5

Draw the wedge profile all around the car.
Draw a straight line across the back of the car at the high point, and in the front of the car at the low point. Connect the points again on the other side.

6

Clamp the block.
Use two quick clamps to secure the block to the work surface so the end of the block is easy to saw. Keep in mind that you'll have to readjust the block every so often or you'll cut into the table.

7

Saw the wedge.
Use a coping saw to follow the reference lines you drew. Starting from the end of the block is easiest. If you get off the line a bit, the surface can be corrected with sanding.

8

Gather the sanding materials.
Grab a sheet of 100-grit sandpaper and
painter's tape. Save the bottom half of the
block for later!

9

Create the sanding station.
Tape the sandpaper down to a hard, flat
surface. Test whatever tape you use to
make sure it will come up without damaging
the work surface.

Don't forget
to pick up a can
of elbow grease!

elbow grease
NET WT. 4 OZ.

SHIFA
SHIFA

10

Sand the top of the car.
Slide the car back and forth over the
sandpaper until the surface is smooth. This
is where you need that can of elbow grease!

Before you ask your mom or dad where they keep the
elbow grease, I'll let you in on a secret. There is no such thing!
"Elbow grease" is what people say when they mean that doing
something will take some hard work!

11

Round over the front edge.
Keeping the full tip of the car flat on the sandpaper, pull the car and change the angle—you'll begin with the car flat on the paper, and end with it nearly vertical.

After the dust settles...

12

Look over your sanding.
The nose of the car has been rounded. Note the nice curve from the top to the flat edge on the bottom.

Sanding the Nose
Start with the top of the car almost flat on the sandpaper. Drag the car toward you, moving it so by the time you end your stroke, the car is vertical. This will make the nose of the car into a nice smooth curve.

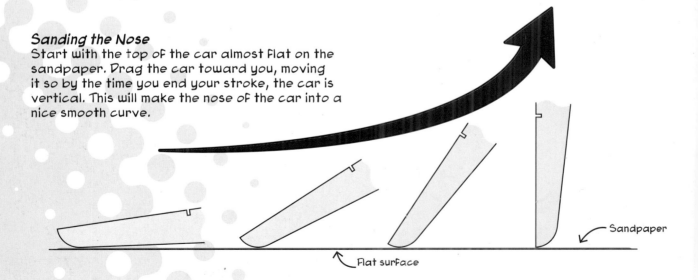

Sandpaper

Flat surface

13

The block is all sanded and ready to be painted!

Soften the edges.
Check out the sidebar below. Lightly sand the entire car and remove any sharp edges.

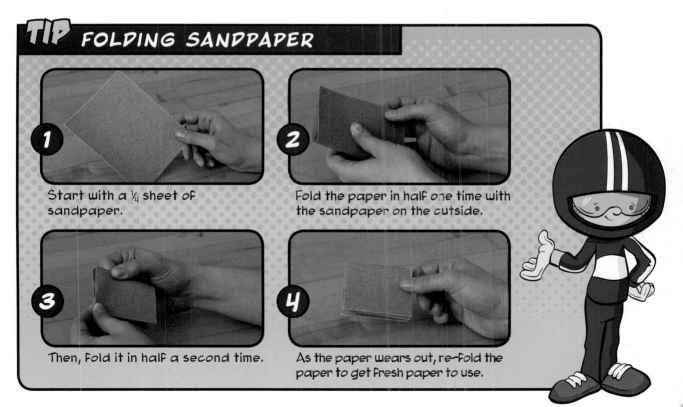

TIP FOLDING SANDPAPER

1 Start with a ¼ sheet of sandpaper.

2 Fold the paper in half one time with the sandpaper on the outside.

3 Then, fold it in half a second time.

4 As the paper wears out, re-fold the paper to get fresh paper to use.

SHAPING OPTIONS

SHAPING WITH POWER TOOLS!

Using a rotary carving tool, such as the Dremel shown here, is a great way to make your car even cooler even quicker. However, you don't need to do this—elbow grease and sandpaper is all you really need (see page 29).

Useful Dremel Bits

| ¼" Sanding Drum (430) | ½" Sanding Drum (407) | Tungsten Carbide Cutter (9933) | Dremel Chuck (4486) |

SHLICK

1

Get the pattern ready.
Cut out the pattern. Put glue on the pattern.

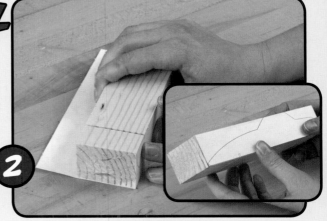

2

Put the pattern on the block.
Line up the block on the paper. Smooth the paper down the sides.

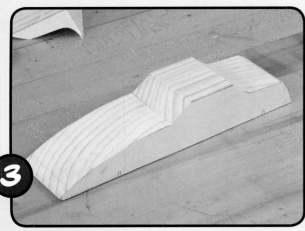

3

Cut out the car.
Use a coping saw to cut out the car.

4

Remove the pattern.
Peel off the pattern. If necessary, sand off any stuck paper.

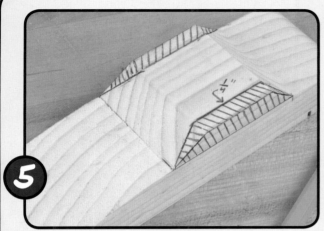

5

Define the roof edge shape.
Measure in ¼" from the sides of the car top. Connect that line diagonally to the edge of the windshield, as shown.

RRRRRR

6

Remove the waste wood.
Use a ½" sanding drum bit on the Dremel to remove the marked wood.

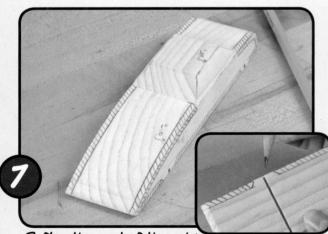

7

Define the rest of the edges.
Measure in ⅛" the rest of the way on the edges of the car. Be careful not to sand away the axle grooves.

8

Rough sand.
Use the ½" sanding drum on the Dremel to rough-sand the waste areas. Remove all of the pencil lined area.

9

Final sanding
Use 220 sandpaper to sand the car. This will remove any fuzzies.

To save time when measuring and marking, first mark the line. Then, position your fingers and pencil on the mark and, keeping your fingers in the same position, run the pencil down the side.

Ten minutes later...

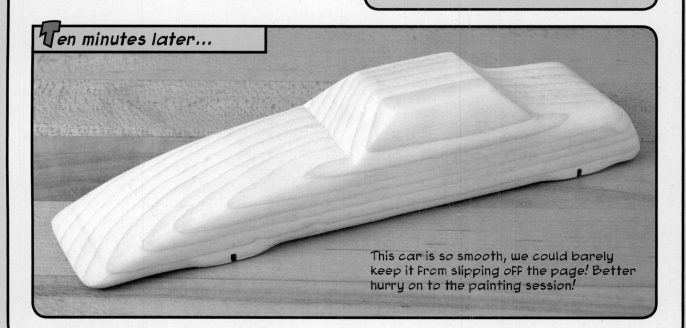

This car is so smooth, we could barely keep it from slipping off the page! Better hurry on to the painting session!

SESSION 3

PAINTING

An Epic Battle of Bland vs Spectacular!

Oops...

THE CHRONICLES OF DASH DERBY

Howdy, Adventurers!

Today I had so much fun painting my car. I think it was the most fun task so far! It has a big racing stripe down the middle that looks really cool, and it wasn't too hard to do. I asked Dad if I could paint a stripe on his car, and he said I could as soon as I became a professional racecar driver. Cool, huh? That'll be about a million years from now, but I bet they'll have super-shiny 3D spaceship paint by then!

Materials & Tool List...

- ☐ 3 – 1" Foam brushes
- ☐ 1" Masking or painter's tape
- ☐ Acrylic paint, colors of your choice
- ☐ Pinstripe tape (optional)
- ☐ Sheet of newspaper
- ☐ Paper plate
- ☐ Sheet of 150-grit sandpaper
- ☐ Scissors
- ☐ 2 popsicle sticks
- ☐ Glue stick
- ☐ Pencil
- ☐ Hair dryer (optional)

1

Assemble the painting materials.
Gather three foam brushes, desired paint colors, masking tape, pinstripes, a paper plate to put the paint on, and newspaper to protect your work surface.

SNIP SNIP

2

Cut tape strips to protect the axle slots.
Rip off a piece of tape about 3" long. Cut the tape in half so it's easier to manage.

3

Round the tape end.
Round the ends of the tape so the strip covers the axle slot edge.

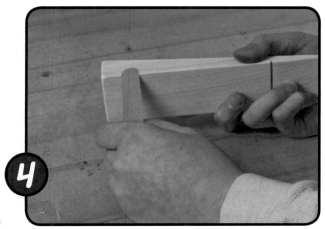

Put the tape over the axle slots.
Cover the axle slots with the tape pieces. Smooth the tape down with your finger to make sure it's firmly attached.

Complete the taping.
Make sure that both axle slots are protected.

Set up the paint station.
Use two foam brushes to elevate the car. Select the color for the stripe and squeeze out a puddle of paint on the paper plate.

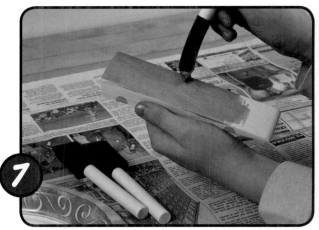

Paint the stripe.
Paint the top of the car the stripe color. Brush front to back. Metallic paint, such as the silver we're using here, will require a couple of coats.

8 half-hour later...

Protect the stripe.
Put a strip of tape over the middle of the car. Press it down firmly to ensure that the edges are secure. What's under the tape will be the stripe.

WHOOSH

9

Paint the bottom of the car.
Pick a color for the body of the car. Hold the car upside down and apply paint around the tape. Brush with the grain.

10

Paint the top of the car.
Put the car on the handles of two foam brushes. Paint the top.

I knew it! Red cars are faster!

ZOOM

FIZZLE

11

Dry the car.
You can use a hairdryer to speed up the drying of the paint. You'll probably need two coats.

12

Remove the tape.
Remove the tape carefully, pulling it vertically to reduce the chance of pulling off paint. Also remove the axle slot tape.

13

Prepare to add pinstripe tape.
Pinstripe tape is ⅛" thick and can be purchased in rolls from hobby shops and auto parts stores.

14

Cut pinstripe tape.
Cut two pieces of pinstripe tape 10" long. Peel off the paper on the back. Center the tape over the paint line—this way, you'll hide any blotting.

SANDING STICKS

Don't stop now... Take a few minutes to build two sanding sticks before you move on to the next session.

1 Gather the materials.
You'll need two popsicle sticks, wood or craft glue, or a gluestick, and a piece of 150-grit sandpaper.

2 Trace the popsicle stick.
Place the stick on the edge of the sandpaper sheet and trace around it. Do this twice.

3 Cut out the sandpaper.
Use old scissors to cut along the pencil marks you just made.

4 Put glue on the sandpaper.
Apply glue to the sandpaper strips.

5 Press onto the stick.
Carefully align the sandpaper over the stick and press it down firmly. Put some newspaper and then a heavy book on top of the stick and let it sit overnight.

Decoration options.
You can decorate your car however you want—go to the craft store and get scrapbook paper; get stickers from the scout store; borrow markers from your parents' stash; get some rub-on decals in the grocery store checkout aisle; grab pinstriping from the auto parts store.

PERMANENT MARKERS

Permanent markers are a quick way to make a custom finish on your car. You can choose from any of the colors in the rainbow, and using markers has the added bonus of still letting the wood grain show through. Make sure you don't get any permanent marker on anything besides your car, though! It is **permanent.**

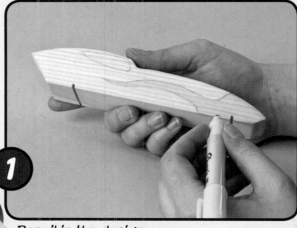

1

Pencil in the design.
Use a pencil to draw on what you want. Then decide what colors to use and start filling in the areas with the lightest colors.

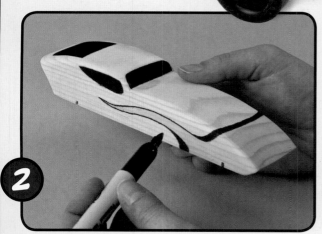

2

Outline the areas.
Use a dark color to outline the light areas. Don't hold the marker in one place too long, or the ink will bleed past the line where you want it. Color the windows in.

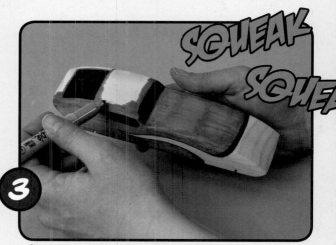

SQUEAK
SQUEAK

3

Add the other colors.
Color in all the other areas that are left. Fill in large areas by drawing with the wood grain. This will keep all the lines going the same way and keep your finish from looking scribbled.

PAINTING OPTIONS

WRAPPING WITH PAPER

Paper is a great way to wrap your car in a colorful pattern. Try wrapping paper, newspaper, scrapbook paper, comic book pages, or whatever else you can find! The instructions for all of them will be the same as you see here.

Gather the materials.
Prepare your car by applying two coats of paint, allowing it to dry, and then sanding the top surface smooth. Get some scrapbook paper, glue, and a foam brush.

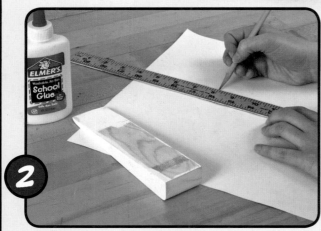

Mark up the paper.
Decide what section of the paper you want to put on your car. Put the car down and trace along both sides. Move the car and use a ruler to extend the lines the whole way to the edge of the paper.

Tape the strip.
Use scissors to cut along the lines you traced. Place the car on the paper and cut off any excess paper. Use a piece of tape to keep the paper aligned on the car.

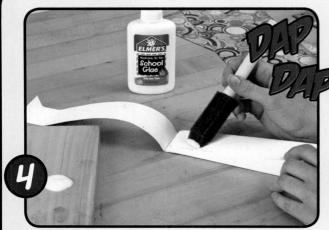

DAP DAP

4

Apply glue.
Put some glue on a scrap of wood or paper. Use a foam brush to apply glue to the top surface of the car.

5

Affix the paper.
Flip the car over so the top is down. Stretch the paper firmly and press the car down to the paper. Glue around the edge and fix the paper to the bottom.

6

Mix the top layer of thinned glue.
Mix 3 parts glue and 1 part water.

7

Apply the thinned glue.
Use a foam brush to apply the thinned glue to the bottom flaps, sides, and top. Wait for it to dry and apply a second coat.

PAINTING OPTIONS

APPLYING DECALS

Decals and stickers are a quick and easy way to customize your car. All you need to do is cut them out and stick them on where you want them.

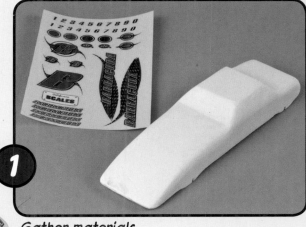

1

Gather materials.
Choose stickers or decals. You can leave the car unpainted, but I think it looks cool to paint it a light color. I painted this car white.

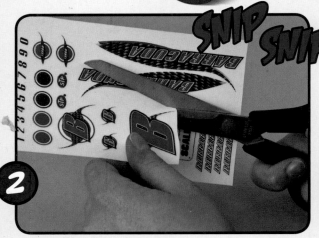

SNIP SNIP

2

Cut out the decals.
You can skip this step if you're using stickers. For decals, cut as close to the edge of the design as you can. This will look better on the car than having lots of extra material around the decal.

3

Attach the decals.
Carefully place the decal or sticker where you want it. Smooth it down so it gets good and stuck to the wood. If you want, you can paint on windows or other details like I did.

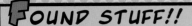

FOUND STUFF!!

Have a look through your toy box; there are probably tons of broken or forgotten-about things in the bottom.

Shark Car
How cool would it be to paint your car like water and glue a shark to the top?

Happy Meal Toys
These are fun to saw apart and glue to a basic car design to give it a custom look.

Army Men
These guys are great! Their bases are very easy to glue on to your car.

Legos
Lego men make great drivers. You could cut a flat green base plate and glue it on top of a car. Then, you could build legos on to the top. Remember, nothing can fall off on the track.

Toy Cars
Great for ideas for car design and shape. Get inspired!

Creatures
Paint your car like dirt or grass and glue a few creatures on the top, or add more stuff and make it look a scene from a movie!

Broken Toy Parts
Dig all the way to the bottom of your toy box. You never know what awesome parts are waiting for you.

Plastic Food
What's funnier than cars with food themes?! Hot dog cars, corn cob cars, pizza cars... the options are endless.

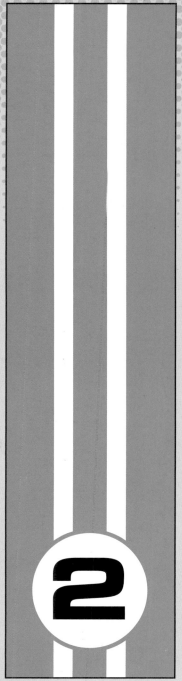

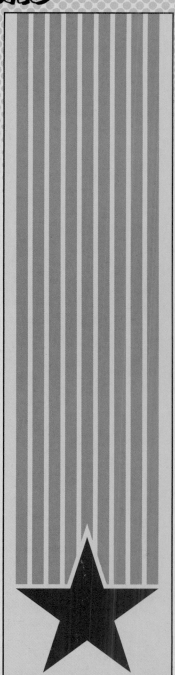

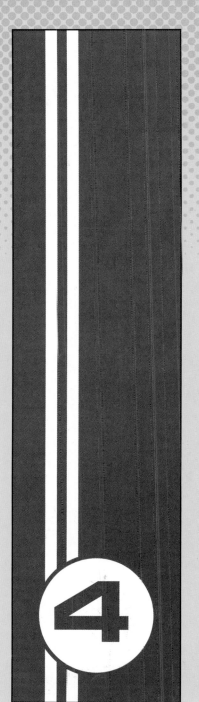

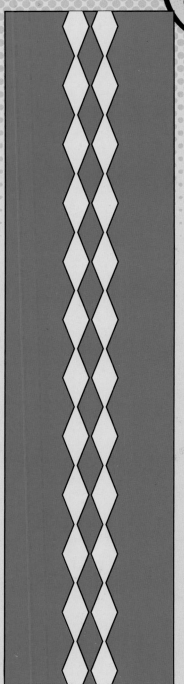

Getting Started in *Pinewood Derby*

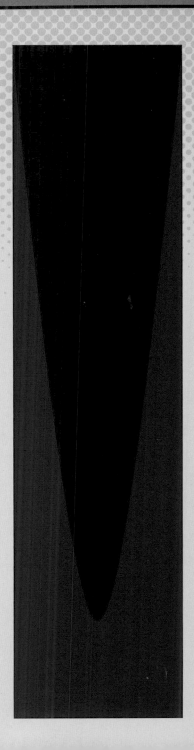

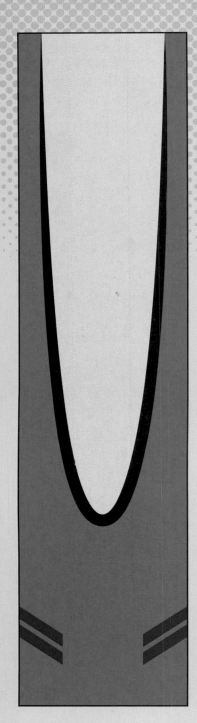
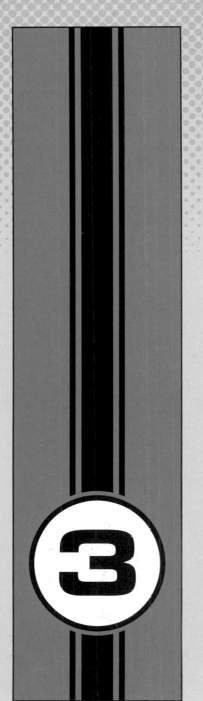

Getting Started in *Pinewood Derby*

SESSION 4
AXLE PREP
The Perils of Polishing

THE CHRONICLES OF DASH DERBY

Ahoy Adventurers!

Today I got the axles for my car nice and shiny. They are polished so well that I can actually see my face in them! If I get close enough, anyway... they are kinda small. Mom says that making the axles so smooth will really help my car go faster by making the meeting places between the axles and wheels extra slippery. She said it's like sliding across the kitchen floor in your socks, instead of sneakers. I don't recommend trying to slide across the floor in sneakers, by the way—you'll just fall down and leave scuff marks on the floor!

Materials & Tool List...

- ☐ 4 Axles
- ☐ Power drill
- ☐ 2 Sanding sticks from page 41
- ☐ Small bowl and water
- ☐ 400-grit wet/dry sandpaper
- ☐ 600-grit wet/dry sandpaper
- ☐ Scissors
- ☐ Paper towels

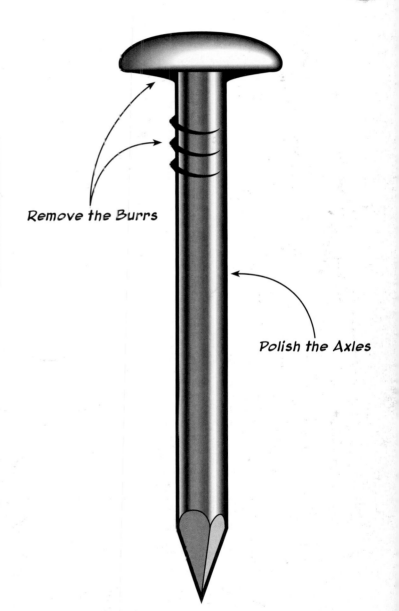

Remove the Burrs

Polish the Axles

1

Chuck the axle into the drill.
Carefully chuck the axle into the drill. It has
to be tight, so you might need a parent's help.

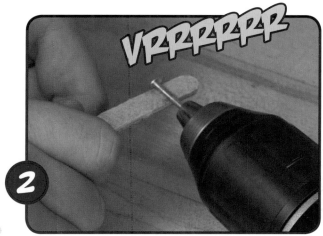

VRRRRRR

2

Sand the axle.
Have a parent hold the drill down and make it go. Use the sanding stick to polish the axle until all three burrs are gone. Repeat on all axles.

3

Sand the underside of the axle head.
There are 2 burrs on the underside of the axle. Turn the sanding stick sideways and polish it until the two burrs are gone. Repeat on all axles.

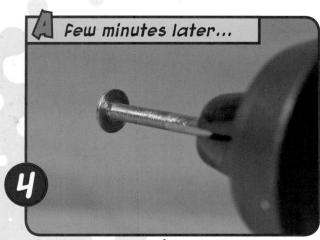

A few minutes later...

4

Burrs are removed!
Now the burrs are gone, but the axle is scratched up.

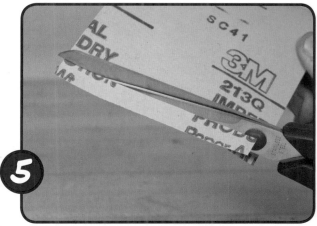

SC41
AL
DRY
3M
213Q

5

Cut the sandpaper into strips.
Cut four strips of ¼"-wide 400-grit wet/dry sandpaper. You'll use these to make the axles nice and smooth.

Wet the sandpaper.
Fill a small bowl with water and dip the sandpaper strips.

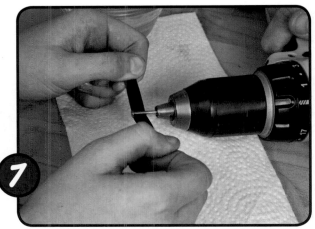

Polish the axle.
Get a paper towel. Hold the sandpaper face up and pull against the axle. Have your parent hold the drill and press the button. Repeat with the rest of the axles.

Polish the edge of the head.
Use the wet sandpaper to polish the edge of the head of the axle. Repeat with the rest of the axles. Repeat with 600-grit sandpaper.

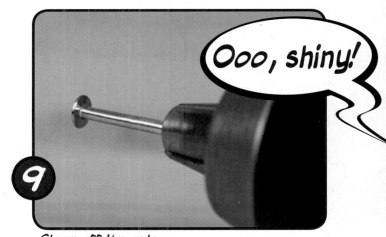

Clean off the axle.
Turn off the drill and rub the axle with a paper towel to clean it off.

SESSION 5
WHEEL PREP
The Revolutionary Adventure Continues

THE CHRONICLES OF DASH DERBY

Hey Adventurers!

Today I got to use some really cool wet/dry sandpaper to polish the wheels of my car. Dad ran the drill so the wheels spun around really fast, and then I got to polish the wheels. Oh! Did I mention that my wheels are orange? My big brother had to use black wheels for his derby car, but I get to use colored ones! I think he's jealous.

Materials & Tool List...

- ☐ 4 Wheels
- ☐ Wheel mandrel
- ☐ Power drill
- ☐ Masking tape
- ☐ 400-grit wet/dry sandpaper
- ☐ Small bowl and water
- ☐ Paper towels
- ☐ Block of wood or the rest of the block from cutting the block in half

Gather the materials.
You'll need the rest of the block from the car, a wheel mandrel, the wheels, wet/dry sandpaper, a drill, and masking tape.

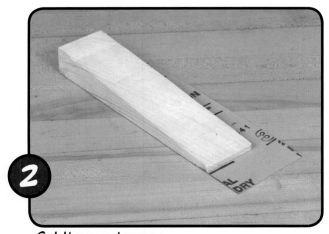

Cut the sandpaper.
Cut the sandpaper so that it's about an inch wider than the block.

Tape the sandpaper.
Tape the sandpaper to the top of the block. Wrap the paper tightly around the block. You've created a sanding block for the wheels.

4

Install the mandrel.
Insert the base of the mandrel into the drill.
Put the outside half of the mandrel through
the wheel, then thread it into the mandrel
base. Don't run the drill while you do this.

5

Set up the wheel sanding station.
Prop the drill on the tape roll to give it some
height. Put down some paper towels under
the sanding block, and have water nearby.

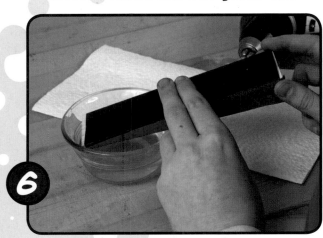

6

Wet the sandpaper.
Wet your fingers and add some water to the
sanding surface.

7

WHIRRRR

Begin polishing the wheels.
Hold the wheel flat. Move the sandpaper
around as your parent slowly powers the
drill. Be sure to keep the sandpaper wet.
Repeat for all wheels.

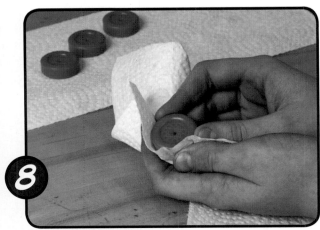

8

Clean off the wheels.

Wash the wheels with soap and water. Clean the inside of the wheel bore. Dry them with a paper towel.

Colored Wheels – Sweet!

Most Pinewood Derby kits come with black wheels, but now you can get other colors. I picked orange for my car, but there were blue ones, red ones, and yellow ones, too—it was hard to choose. Maybe the next car I make, I'll use one of each color. What color will you pick? You could really make your car look cool by matching or contrasting the color of the car and the wheels. All these colors remind me of a joke: What color is a belch? Burple!

WEIGHTING

The Fate of Your Car Hangs in the Balance

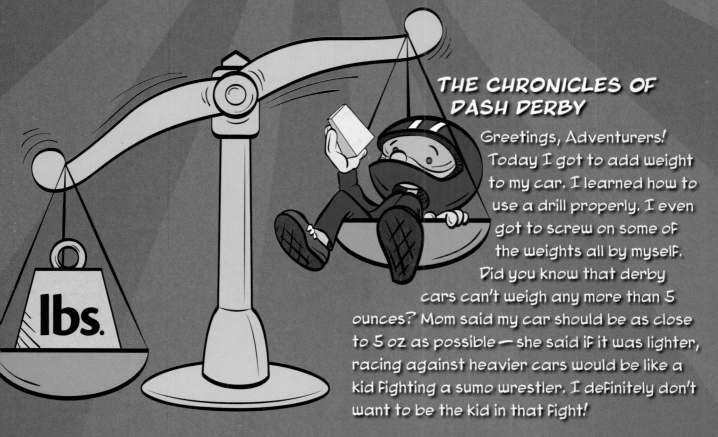

THE CHRONICLES OF DASH DERBY

Greetings, Adventurers! Today I got to add weight to my car. I learned how to use a drill properly. I even got to screw on some of the weights all by myself. Did you know that derby cars can't weigh any more than 5 ounces? Mom said my car should be as close to 5 oz as possible — she said if it was lighter, racing against heavier cars would be like a kid fighting a sumo wrestler. I definitely don't want to be the kid in that fight!

Materials & Tool List...

- ☐ Scale
- ☐ Painted car body
- ☐ 4 Wheels
- ☐ 4 Axles
- ☐ Weight plate
- ☐ Small split shot
- ☐ Power drill with ½" drill bit
- ☐ Paper towels
- ☐ Masking or painters' tape
- ☐ Cardboard
- ☐ Scissors
- ☐ Permanent marker
- ☐ Pencil
- ☐ Small screwdriver
- ☐ Graphite

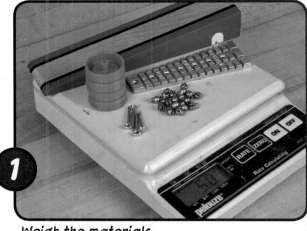

1

Weigh the materials.
The body weighs 1.7 oz. The wheels are .4 oz. The axles are .1 oz. The weight plate is 2.1 oz. All together, the materials weigh 4.3 oz. We need more weight to get it up to 5 oz., so add split shot.

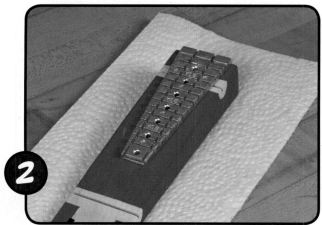

2

Prepare the car.
Put the car upside down on a soft surface to protect it. Put the weight plate on the bottom of the car so the edge of it is touching the very back. It is important to keep the weight as far back as possible.

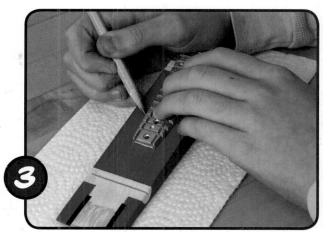

3

Trace the plate.
Trace around the weight plate with a pencil.

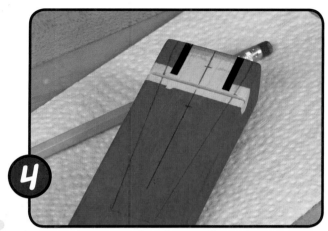

4

Mark the holes for the split shot.
Draw a centerline down the middle of the car. Mark 7/16" toward the front and back from the rear axle slot.

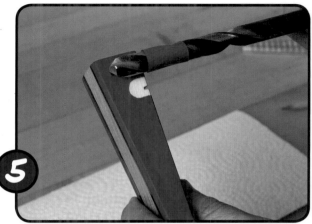

5

Mark bit to drill the first hole.
Hold the drill bit up to the side of the car. Use some tape to mark the depth you want the hole to be. It shouldn't be any closer than 1/8" to the top.

WHIRRRR

6

Drill holes for split shot.
Use as large of a drill bit as you have (I use 1/2") to drill a hole in the back of the car for the split shot.

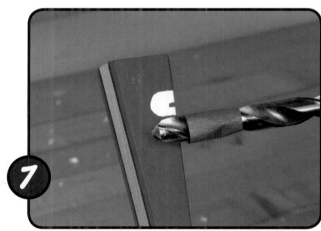

7

Re-mark the bit for the second hole.
Repeat Step 5 for the second hole—it will be a different depth, but make sure it is still no closer to the top than 1/8".

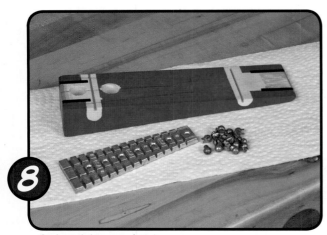

Get out the weights.
All the weights are ready to be inserted.

Add the split shot.
Put the split shot in the holes.

SMASH!

Flatten the split shot.
If the split shot protrudes from the hole, use the handle of the foam brush and a hammer to flatten the shot. Don't glue in the shot; that way, you can just unscrew the plate and remove a few if you're over 5 oz at the race.

Attach the plate.
Put the plate back on the car and attach it with its two screws. Use the tip of a nail or an awl to start the screws.

12

Create a spacer for the wheels.
Cut out a piece of cardboard from the Pinewood Derby kit box. Tape together two pieces of the cardboard. Cut a small notch, and now you have a spacer for the wheels.

13

Gather the materials to add the wheels.
You'll need your car, the wheels, the axles, a permanent marker, and the wheel spacers.

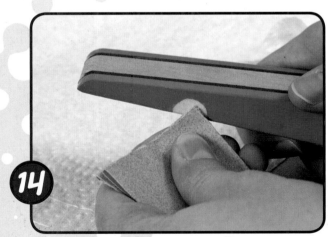

14

Sand the axle groove.
Use 220 sandpaper to sand the area on the side of the car next to the axle groove.

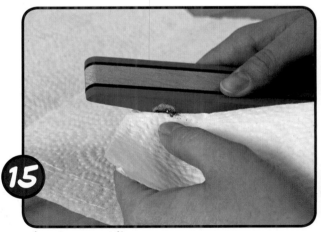

15

Apply graphite.
Use a paper towel to rub in graphite onto the side of the car where the wheels will rub.

Insert the wheels.
Put the car on its side. Place the spacer next to the axle slot. Push the axle through the wheel and push the head of the axle with the end of the marker until the wheel is snug to the spacer.

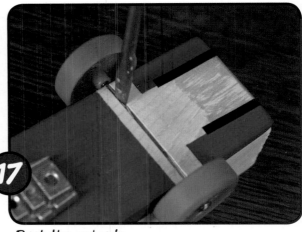

Push the axles in.
Use a flat blade screwdriver to put the axles the whole way in the axle slots.

Look over the car.
When you've inserted all the wheels and axles, take a quick look at the bottom of the car to make sure it looks like this, with everything aligned the right way.

When is a car not a car? When it turns into a driveway!

SESSION 7
TEST RUNS
The Daring and Heroic Art of Fine-Tuning

THE CHRONICLES OF DASH DERBY

Dear Adventurers,
Today was so exciting—I got to take my car on some test runs! Mom wasn't super-happy about us running the car on her dining room table, but that made it even more fun! One word of warning...if you need to apply some extra graphite to the axles, make sure you do it outside, or the mess might be too much for your mom to take!

Materials & Tool List...

- ☐ Table leaf or long, flat board
- ☐ Place mat or other soft, thick cloth
- ☐ Masking or painter's tape
- ☐ Level
- ☐ Permanent marker
- ☐ Small flat screwdriver
- ☐ Hammer
- ☐ Graphite

1

Gather the materials.
Grab an extra table leaf and raise it about 2 ½" on one end. You'll also need painter's tape and something to soften the car's landing.

2

Apply tape.
Use the painter's tape to make a track about 5" wide the whole way down the leaf.

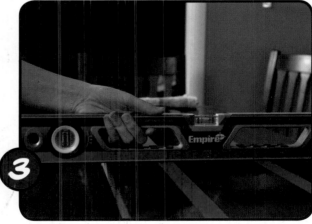

3

Level the leaf.
Use a level to make sure the leaf is level from side to side. If it isn't, your car will roll off the sides into oblivion!

Add crash pad.
Find something soft—a pillow, a rolled up place mat, whatever—to serve as a stop at the bottom of the ramp.

Get set!
Put the car in the middle of the track at the top.

The first run...

WEEEEE!

Go!
Let go of the car. If you're super-lucky, the car will go straight down the middle of the test track and you can skip to Step 14. If the car went right or left, we need to fix it!

Find the wheel that steers.
Place the car on a flat surface. Put your finger on the front center. As you push down, the car will shift toward one of the wheels. The other wheel carries the weight. You'll need to know this to continue.

Mark the steering axle.
Pull out the axle and wheel that you just figured out carries the weight. Mark the axle where it comes out of the wheel.

Darken the line.
Use your permanent marker to darken the line around the axle.

Set up the axle corrector.
Get two things that you can sit the axle on.

Bend the axle.
Use a flat head screwdriver and a hammer to very lightly tap the axle at the mark you made. Lightly!

TEST RUNS

CRUNCH!

12

Good and bad.
When you are done (lightly!) bending the axle, it should look like the one on top. If it looks like the one on the bottom, start over with a new axle, and tap lighter this time!

13

Mark the 12 o'clock position.
Reinsert the wheel and axle into the car so the axle is bent upward. Use a permanent marker to mark the 12 o'clock position. This is where 12 o'clock is on a dial clock.

Do a test run!

If your car curves left:
Rotate your steering axle counter-clockwise 45°. See the top illustration on the next page.

If your car goes straight down the middle:
Don't touch a thing! You're ready to go!

If your car curves right:
Rotate your steering axle clockwise 45°. See the bottom illustration on the next page.

If your car curves left...

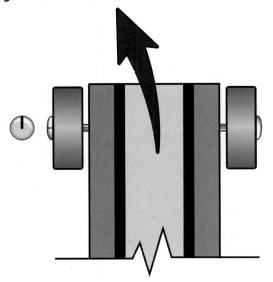

...Rotate the axle counter-clockwise 45°. This tilts the axle bend forward.

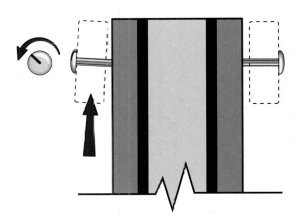

If your car curves right...

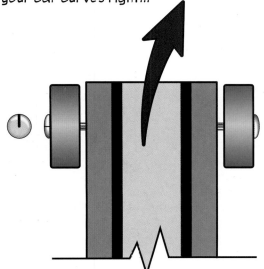

...Rotate the axle clockwise 45°. This tilts the axle bend backward.

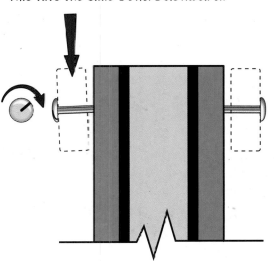

Car Alignment Tests

Test Run #1	Test Run #2	Test Run #3	Test Run #4
☐ Car pulls to the right ☐ Car pulls to the left ☐ Stays in the center	☐ Car pulls to the right ☐ Car pulls to the left ☐ Stays in the center	☐ Car pulls to the right ☐ Car pulls to the left ☐ Stays in the center	☐ Car pulls to the right ☐ Car pulls to the left ☐ Stays in the center
Axle Angle: Record the angle of your axle here ⟶ ◯	Axle Angle: ◯	Axle Angle: ◯	Axle Angle: ◯
Notes:	Notes:	Notes:	Notes:

Car Alignment Tests

Test Run #5	Test Run #6	Test Run #7	Test Run #8
☐ Car pulls to the right ☐ Car pulls to the left ☐ Stays in the center	☐ Car pulls to the right ☐ Car pulls to the left ☐ Stays in the center	☐ Car pulls to the right ☐ Car pulls to the left ☐ Stays in the center	☐ Car pulls to the right ☐ Car pulls to the left ☐ Stays in the center
Axle Angle: ◯	Axle Angle: ◯	Axle Angle: ◯	Axle Angle: ◯
Notes:	Notes:	Notes:	Notes:

PUFF PUFF

14

Apply graphite inside the wheel.
Gently squeeze the graphite into the space on the axle between the car body and the wheel. Put down a paper towel to contain the mess.

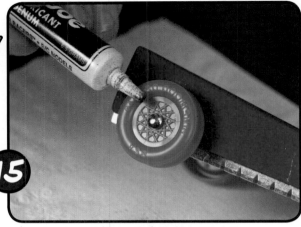

15

Apply graphite outside the wheel.
Squeeze some more graphite on the axle between the head and the wheel.

TIP BREAKING IN THE WHEELS

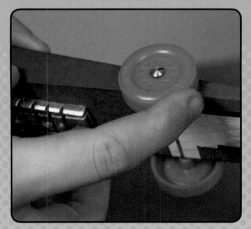

One of the best tips for making your car run smoothly is breaking in the wheels. The easiest way to do this is to spin the wheels with your finger. As you spin each wheel, the graphite will work into the nooks and crannies and make everything smooth and polished. The smoother and more polished the axle is, the faster your car will go! It's a good idea to watch a TV show or movie while you do this, because you can spend 15 minutes or so per wheel if you want. While you spin the wheels, be careful not to bump the alignment too much. You'll probably need to do another test run afterward to make sure everything is lined up, but you don't want to do any damage while you're breaking in the wheels. Spin carefully!

RACE DAY TIPS
The Final Frontier

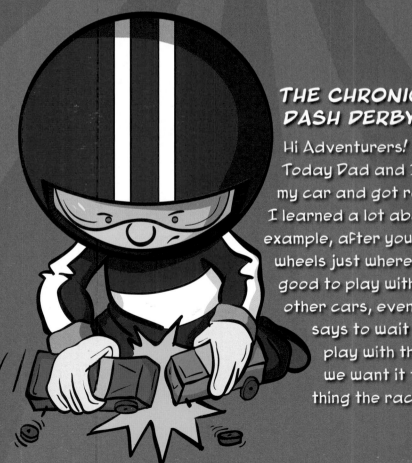

THE CHRONICLES OF DASH DERBY

Hi Adventurers!
Today Dad and I took a last look at my car and got ready for the big race. I learned a lot about what not to do! For example, after you get your car axles and wheels just where you want them, it is not good to play with the car or smash it into other cars, even though that is fun. Dad says to wait until after the race to play with the car, or it won't do what we want it to during the race. Good thing the race is tomorrow!

Weigh-in: When you get to the race, you'll have to weigh your car to prove that it weighs the correct five ounces. Here's a method to practice at home. Put your scale on the table and carefully place the car on the scale. It is important to put the car on the scale upside down—that way, your car can't roll off and mess up your wheel alignment. Add small weights to the scale until it reads exactly 5.0 ounces. Then, add those weights to the car. If you practice this, when you show up at weigh-in, you'll know exactly what to do.

Be prepared: Bring a small screwdriver to remove the weight plate if you need to add more split shot during weigh-in.

Storage: Store your finished car in a zipper gallon-size bag before the race. This will keep your wheels clean, so they run smoothly. There are a lot of tips here that will help you keep your car wheels and axles clean—it is very important!

Clean hands: Make sure your hands are clean before holding your car, especially if you just ate a donut! All that sticky stuff will mess up your wheels and make your car run slower.

Holding the car: Don't hold your car by the wheels. Hold it by the center. You don't want to mess up all the work you just did to get the wheels rolling super-fast!

Not a toy—yet: Never roll your car on any surface before the race—especially the floor. Dirt will stick to your wheels and slow your car down. Wait until after the races are over before you play with your car!

Line it up: When you put your car on the track to race, make sure the wheels are completely in the lane and not sitting up on the lane guides. If not, your car could crash during the race.

Graphite: Bring graphite or lube, just in case. If you drop the car, or get the wheels dirty, you might be able to clean off the wheels and make the wheel/axle meeting place slippery again. Plus, I always like to have stuff on hand to help other racers. Maybe some of your friends don't know about using graphite, and you can help them out.

Superglue to the rescue: Having superglue with you is always a good idea. You never know if something is going to fall off, or if a friend's car might fall apart. You can save the day, with the help of Super Glue!

What to bring to the big race:
- ☐ Small screwdriver
- ☐ Extra split shot
- ☐ Extra graphite or lube
- ☐ Super glue
- ☐ Tape
- ☐ Camera or video camera
- ☐ Money for snacks
- ☐ This book and a pen to record your race times

Wow! If you've never seen a derby racing track before, your first thought will probably be something like..."Wow, that's long!" It's the perfect place to race the cars you just made, and it's a lot of fun to watch.

MEMORIES
Documenting Your Exploits

THE CHRONICLES OF DASH DERBY

Hey there, Adventurers!

Today I got to race my car! I got 3rd place in the first race, 1st in the second, and 2nd in the third. I even got to go to the Finals! My car was third best out of the whole group! Everybody's cars were really cool, and fast, too. I already have an idea for next year's car. Mom made me a bunch of scrapbook pages to fill in with my photos and cool stuff about the race. Check out the next few pages and fill in the blanks with your own stuff! That way, you can keep your own chronicle of your derby race.

Place a photo of your finished derby car

Race Details:

Date _____

Location _____

Number of competitors _____

Race Car Details:

Car Number _____

How long did it take to build? _____

Favorite detail on your car_____
_____

Finishing positions:

Race #1 _____

Race #2 _____

Race #3 _____

Finals _____

Favorite memory:

_____
_____
_____
_____

MEMORIES

Place a photo of building your car

Place a photo of building your car

Place a photo of building your car

Race #1				
Lane Number	Lane # 1	Lane # 2	Lane # 3	Lane # 4
Time				
Position				

Race #2				
Lane Number	Lane # 1	Lane # 2	Lane # 3	Lane # 4
Time				
Position				

Race #3				
Lane Number	Lane # 1	Lane # 2	Lane # 3	Lane # 4
Time				
Position				

Did you advance to the Final Round?　❏ Yes　❏ No

Final Round				
Lane Number	Lane # 1	Lane # 2	Lane # 3	Lane # 4
Time				
Position				

PATTERNS
Journey to the Lost Temple of Car Designs

THE CHRONICLES OF DASH DERBY

Hi Adventurers! I remember the day I picked out my car design. It is so much fun looking through all the patterns and imagining what you can make with each of them. I finally picked the Basic Wedge, page 81. It is a great design! Look through and pick one you like. Remember this important rule: You can pick your car design, and you can pick your friends, but you can't pick your friends' noses!

Basic Wedge

Cut out this pattern and wrap it around your block →

Waste area

Fold along dotted line

Fold along dotted line

Waste area

Cut along this line →

← Sand the front round

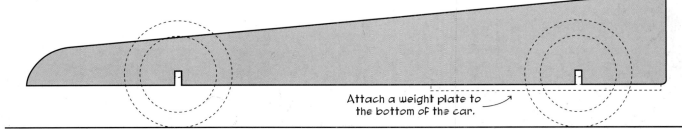

Attach a weight plate to the bottom of the car.

Super Wedge

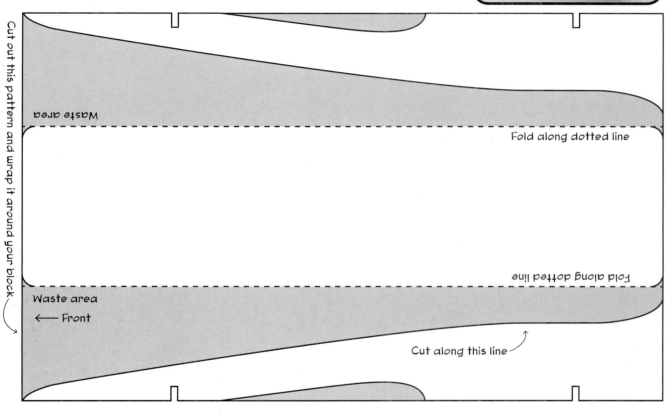

Cut out this pattern and wrap it around your block

Waste area

Fold along dotted line

Fold along dotted line

Waste area

← Front

Cut along this line

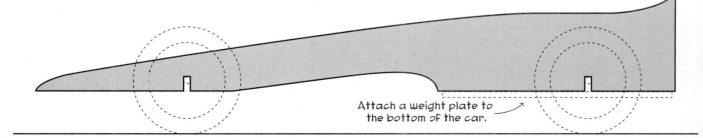

Attach a weight plate to the bottom of the car.

Wave Racer

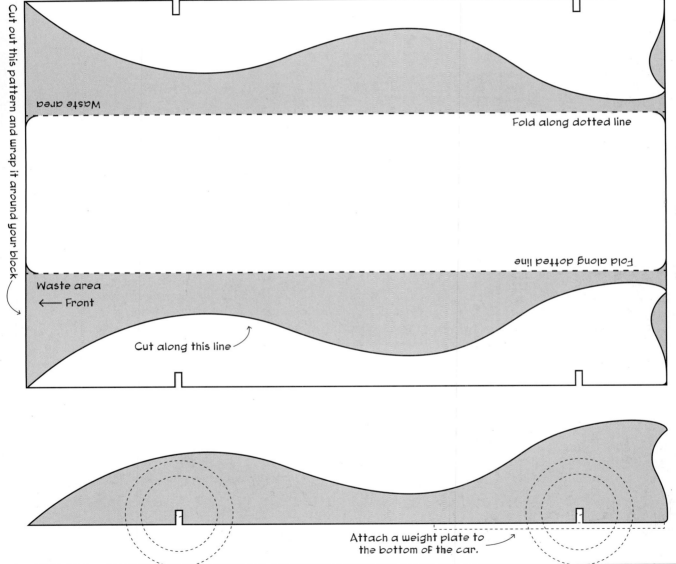

Cut out this pattern and wrap it around your block

Waste area

Fold along dotted line

Fold along dotted line

Waste area

← Front

Cut along this line

Attach a weight plate to the bottom of the car.

Classic Drag Racer

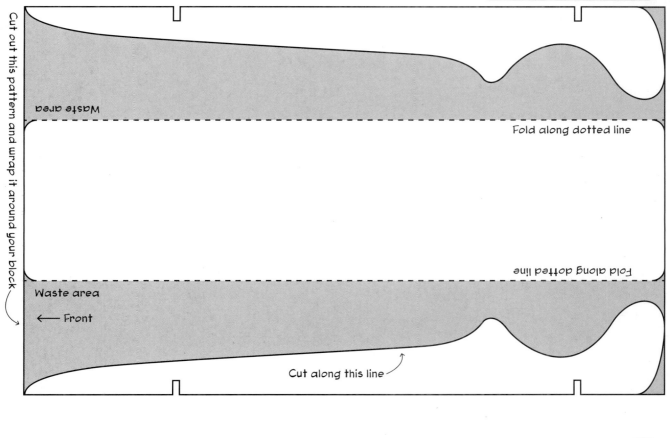

Cut out this pattern and wrap it around your block

Waste area

Fold along dotted line

Fold along dotted line

Waste area

← Front

Cut along this line

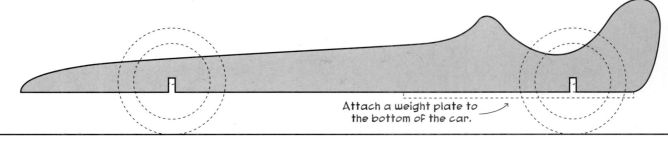

Attach a weight plate to the bottom of the car.

Skate Racer

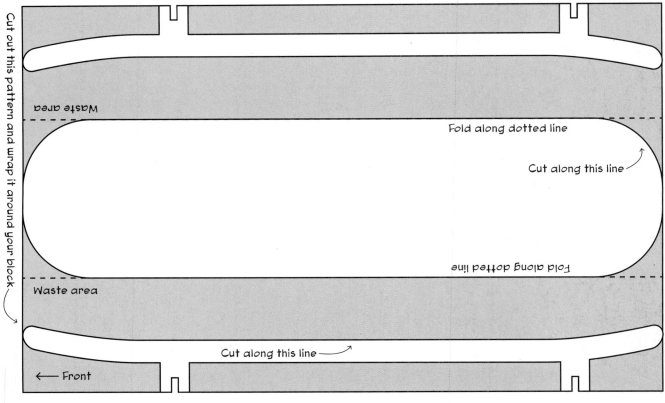

Cut out this pattern and wrap it around your block

Waste area

Fold along dotted line

Cut along this line

Fold along dotted line

Waste area

Cut along this line

← Front

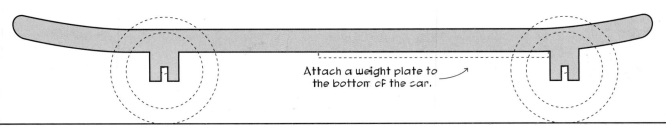

Attach a weight plate to the bottom of the car.

Speed Car

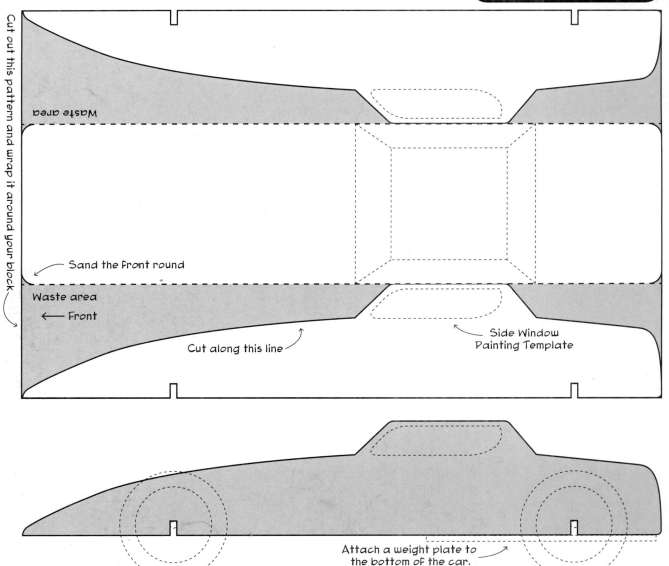

Cut out this pattern and wrap it around your block

Waste area

Sand the front round

Waste area

← Front

Cut along this line

Side Window
Painting Template

Attach a weight plate to
the bottom of the car.

Open Racer

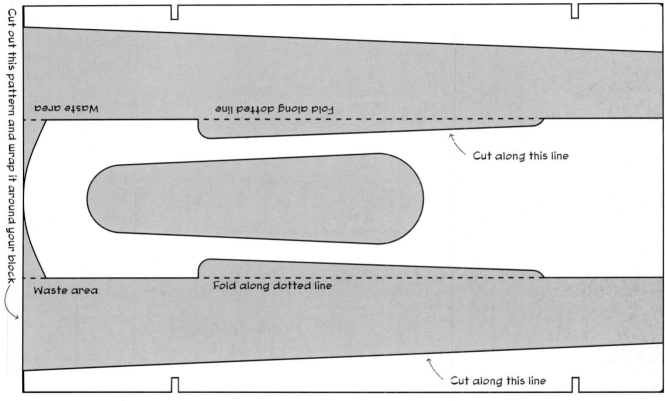

Cut out this pattern and wrap it around your block

Waste area

Fold along dotted line

Cut along this line

Waste area

Fold along dotted line

Cut along this line

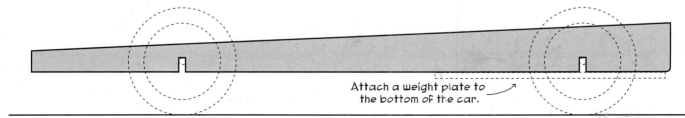

Attach a weight plate to the bottom of the car.

Coupe Racer

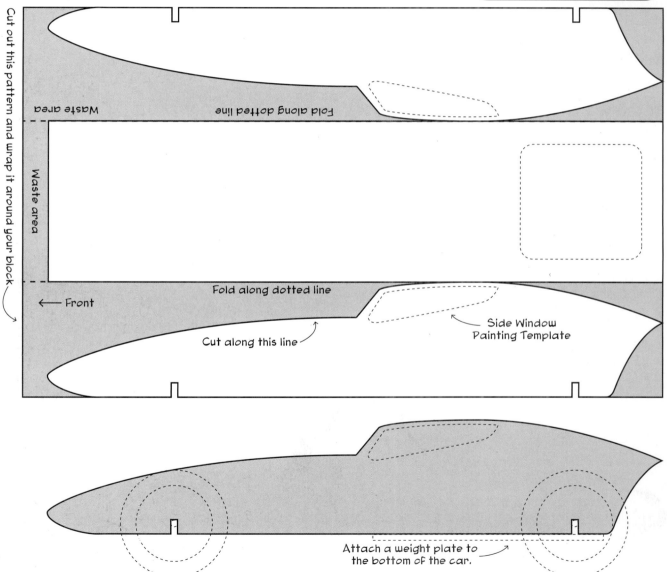

Cut out this pattern and wrap it around your block

Waste area

Waste area

Fold along dotted line

Fold along dotted line

← Front

Cut along this line →

Side Window
Painting Template

Attach a weight plate to
the bottom of the car.

Pickup Truck Speedway

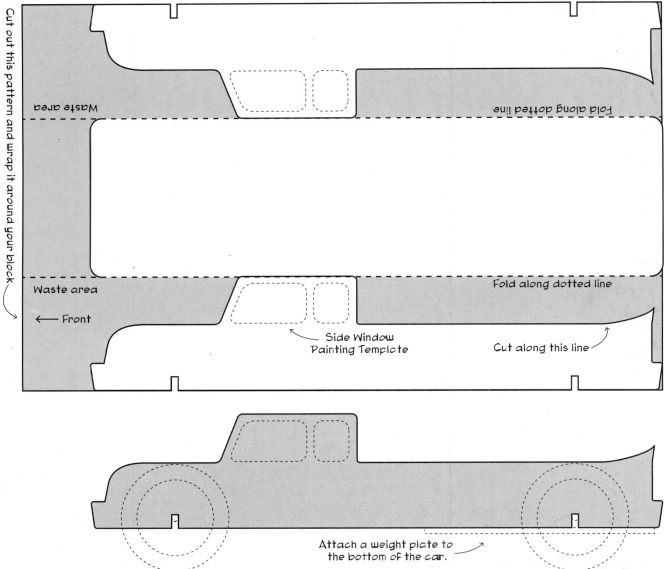

Cut out this pattern and wrap it around your block

Waste area

Fold along dotted line

Waste area

← Front

Side Window
Painting Template

Fold along dotted line

Cut along this line

Attach a weight plate to
the bottom of the car.

Finned Racer

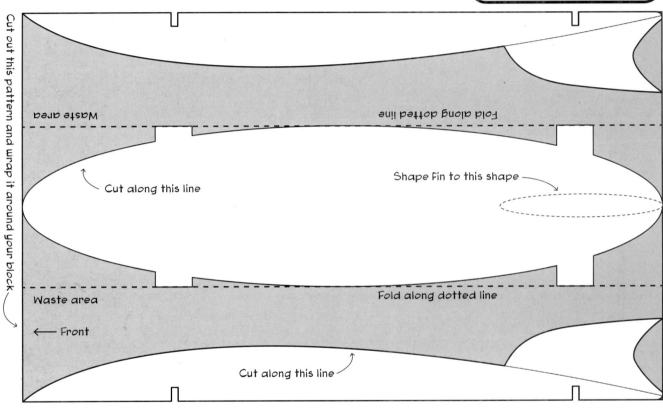

Cut out this pattern and wrap it around your block

Waste area

Fold along dotted line

Cut along this line

Shape Fin to this shape

Waste area

Fold along dotted line

← Front

Cut along this line

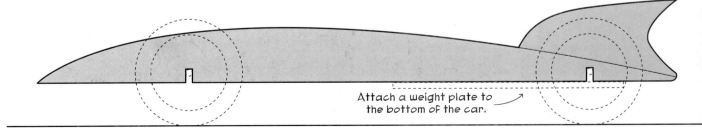

Attach a weight plate to the bottom of the car.

Speed Bump

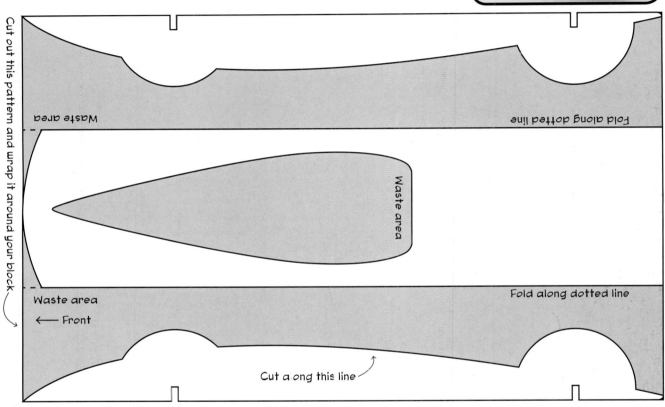

Cut out this pattern and wrap it around your block

Waste area

Fold along dotted line

Waste area

Waste area

← Front

Fold along dotted line

Cut along this line

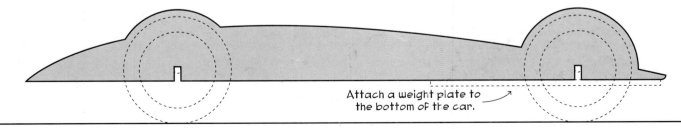

Attach a weight plate to the bottom of the car.

Speed Wedge

Waste area

Fold along dotted line

Waste area

Fold along dotted line

← Front

Cut along this line

Cut out this pattern and wrap it around your block

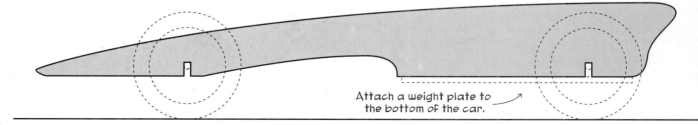

Attach a weight plate to the bottom of the car.

Blank Template

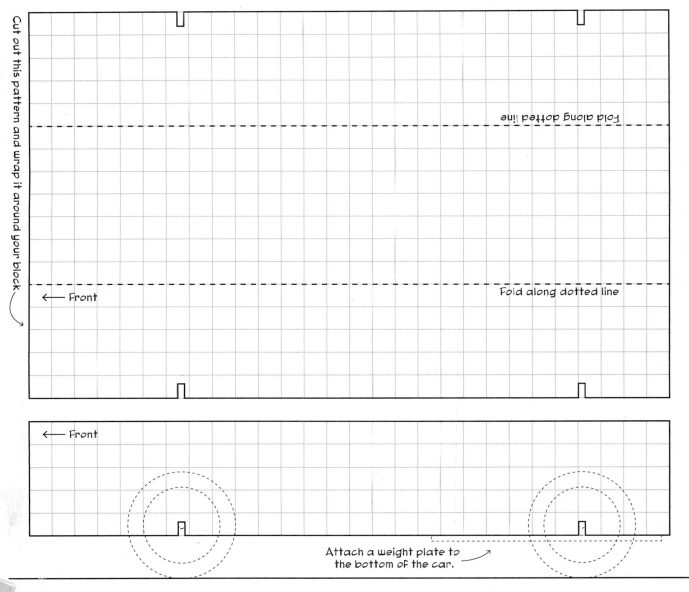

Cut out this pattern and wrap it around your block

Fold along dotted line

Fold along dotted line

← Front

← Front

Attach a weight plate to the bottom of the car.

Getting Started in **Pinewood Derby**

93

Index

adults, guidelines for, 9
axles, 52–55. *See also* wheels
    applying graphite on, 73
    correcting curving cars/alignment
        problems, 68–72
    installing, 64–65
    marking and bending, 69–70
    materials/tools list, 53
    prep steps (sanding and polishing),
        53–55
    sanding groove for, 64
    special tools for, 25

caring for car, 75
coping saw
    curved cuts with, 19
    illustrated, 16
    internal cuts with, 21
    notched cuts with, 20
    skills, 18–21
    straight cuts with, 18
curving cars, correcting, 68–72
cutting wood. *See* coping saw

decals, 46
design, choosing, 12–13. *See also* patterns
documenting memories, 76–79
dust masks, 14

ear protection, 15
eye protection, 14

found stuff, 47

glue supplies, 23, 24, 75
graphite, 23, 24, 64, 73, 75

holding car, 75

inspection rule, 13

kids, cool stuff for, 8

lead warning, 14
lining up car, 75

markers (permanent), 23, 24, 25, 43, 65, 69
measuring shortcut, 35
memories, documenting, 76–79

painting, 36–51. *See also* markers
    (permanent)
    decals and, 46
    design ideas, 48–51

found stuff for ideas, 47
    materials/tools list, 37
    options, 42–47
    step-by-step instructions, 37–40
    supplies for. *See* shopping
    wrapping with paper instead of,
        44–45
paper, wrapping car with, 44–45
parents, guidelines for, 9
patterns, 80–93
    about: applying/using, 33; choosing
        design, 12–13
    basic wedge, 81
    blank template for, 93
    classic drag racer, 84
    coupe racer, 88
    finned racer, 90
    open racer, 87
    pickup truck speedway, 89
    skate racer, 85
    speed bump, 91
    speed car, 86
    speed wedge, 92
    super wedge, 82
    wave racer, 83
pinstripe tape, 23, 24, 37, 40, 42
power tool day, 15. *See also* tools

race day tips, 74–75. *See also*
        documenting memories
rules
    for adults, 9
    for kids, 8
    official Pinewood Derby, 13

safety precautions, 14–15
sanding
    axle, 54–55
    block for, 57–58
    final, 35
    folding sandpaper, 31
    nose, 30
    rotary carving tool for, 32, 34
    safety precautions, 14
    sandpaper for, 23, 24
    shaping steps, 29, 31, 35
    softening edges, 31
    sticks for, 41
    wet, 55, 58
    wheels, 58
scrapbook, 76–79
scrapbook paper, 25, 42, 44
shaping, 26–35. *See also* patterns;
        sanding

cutting wood. *See* coping saw
    options, 34–35
    patterns for. *See* patterns
    step-by-step instructions, 28–31
    supplies for. *See* shopping; tools
shopping, 22–25
    checklists, 23
    stuff needed, illustrated, 24–25
specifications, 13
springs rule, 13
starting out, 10–21. *See also* tools
    choosing design, 12–13
    safety precautions, 14–15
    treasure map of steps, 11
    workspace, 15
steering axle, finding and adjusting, 68–71
steps, treasure map of, 11
storing car, 75
supplies. *See* shopping; tools

test runs, 66–73
    alignment test logs, 72
    finding/fixing causes of right- or left-
        curving cars, 68–72
    materials/tools list, 67
    step-by-step instructions, 67–73
tools. *See also* coping saw
    learning to use, 15
    needed, 16–17
    power tool day, 15
    rotary carving tool, 32, 34
    special, 25
treasure map of steps, 11

weigh-in, 75
weighting, 23, 60–65
    materials/tools list, 61
    step-by-step instructions, 61–65
    weight options, 23
wheels, 56–59. *See also* axles
    applying graphite to, 73
    colored (optional), 22, 23, 59
    finding/fixing alignment problems, 68–72
    installing, 64–65
    materials/tools list, 57
    prep steps, 57–59
    rules, 13
    special tools for, 25
    specification requirements, 13
wood putty, 23, 24
workspace, 15

COPY EDITORS: Paul Hambke and Heather Stauffer   **COVER AND LAYOUT DESIGNER:** Troy Thorne
EDITOR AND COPYWRITER: Kerri Landis   **ILLUSTRATOR:** Jason Deller   **INDEXER:** Jay Kreider   **PROOFREADER:** Lynda Jo Runkle
STEP-BY-STEP HAND MODELS: Kerri Landis and Nathan Thorne   **STEP-BY-STEP PHOTOGRAPHER:** Scott Kriner

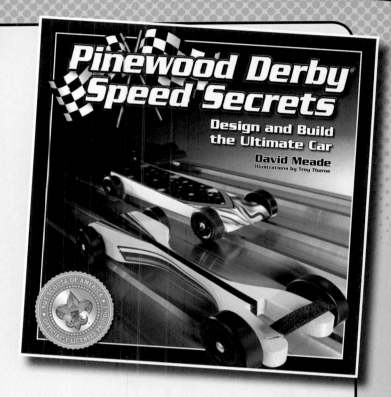

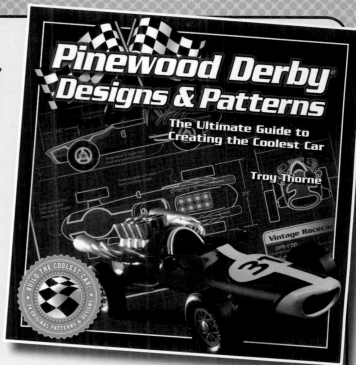